FORENSIC SCIENCE

Identifying Criminals and Victims

Carol Ballard

W

FRANKLIN WATTS

LONDON•SYDNEY

This edition first published in 2010
Franklin Watts
338 Euston Road
London NW1 3BH

Franklin Watts Australia
Level 17/207 Kent Street
Sydney, NSW 2000

A CIP catalogue record for this book is
available from the British Library.

ISBN: 978 0 7496 9499 9

Dewey number: 363.2'58

Printed in Malaysia

Franklin Watts is a division of
Hachette Children's Books,
an Hachette UK company.
www.hachette.co.uk

Note to parents and teachers
concerning websites:
In the book every effort has been made by
the Publishers to ensure that websites are
suitable for children, that they are of the
highest educational value and that they
contain no inappropriate or offensive
material. However, because of the nature of
the Internet, it is impossible to guarantee that
the contents of these sites will not be altered.
We advise that Internet access is supervised by
a responsible adult.

For The Brown Reference Group Ltd
Project Editor: Sarah Eason
Designer: Paul Myerscough
Picture Researcher: Maria Joannou
Managing Editor: Miranda Smith
Editorial Director: Lindsey Lowe
Production Director: Alastair Gourlay
Children's Publisher: Anne O'Daly

Photographic Credits:
Science Photo Library: TEK Image front cover;
Alamy Images: John Angerson 34,
Ian Miles-Flashpoint Pictures 11; Corbis: Steve
Liss 33; Dreamstime: Arkadiusz Fajer 24,
Red2000 9; Fotolia: Paco Ayala 13, David Shyr
25; Getty Images: Fred Dufour/AFP 38,
Mark Renders 43, Taxi/Stephen Simpson 20;
Istockphoto: Kevin Chesson 22, David Elfstrom
23, Emrah Turudu 18; Rex Features: 4, 35,
Eddie Mulholland 29; Science Photo Library:
Mauro Fermariello 36, Pasieka 19;
Shutterstock: Adrian Britton 16, Viktor Gmyria
30, Douglas R Hess 15, Catherine Jones 31,
Ragne Kabanova 6, Emin Kuliyev 5, 21, Milos
Luzanin 7, Tyler Olson 41, Mike Palazzotto 37,
Pokaz 10, Olivier Le Queinec 17, Alexander
Raths 45, Loren Rodgers 42, Dale A Stork 28,
Lee Torrens 8, Elena Uspenskaya 14,
Yakobchuk Vasyl 27.

Contents

Who is it?

henever a crime is discovered, investigators need to identify who the victim is and the criminal who committed the crime.

Who is guilty, who is not?

It is sometimes plainly obvious that a person is guilty of a crime. If one person attacks another, the attacker is the perpetrator of the crime and the person who is attacked is the victim. However, not all cases are this straightforward. If a driver knocks down a pedestrian and does not stop, how can he or she be identified? If a skeleton is found buried in a garden, how can investigators discover how the person died?

4

Crime-scene investigators search a crime scene in minute detail for any evidence that may identify a criminal.

A forensic chemist analyses the evidence brought in from the crime scene. ➡

5

Collecting clues

It is the job of crime-scene investigators to collect every scrap of evidence from a crime scene. Some of the clues can be interpreted on the spot. Other evidence must be sent to the forensic laboratory for analysis. This may help investigators to discover exactly what happened at the crime scene. Other clues will help them to identify both the victim and the criminal.

Analysis

Different tests are carried out at the laboratory, depending on the type of evidence involved. Biological materials such as hairs, cigarette ends and bloodstains may be analysed for DNA. Surfaces are searched for fingerprints. Telephone messages may be analysed for clues that a person's voice may give. Any paper found with writing on may be sent for handwriting analysis.

Sometimes one piece of evidence can be enough to identify an individual. More often, several different pieces of evidence are used together to confirm a person's identity. It is like putting together the pieces of a complicated jigsaw puzzle.

A post mortem is an examination of a dead body. When a body is found, it is photographed at the crime scene. This records exactly how the body and other things were arranged at the scene. Once this is done, the hands and feet are put into bags to preserve evidence on them. The body is put into a body bag and taken to a morgue.

At the morgue

The body is photographed at the morgue, clothes are removed and the body is weighed and measured. Details of sex, race and estimated age are recorded. The pathologist then begins the post mortem to determine when the person died. After death, the body goes through a sequence of changes known as algor, rigor and livor mortis. Algor mortis is when the body cools to the temperature of the surroundings. Rigor mortis is the chemical changes in the body, making it stiffen first and then, some hours later, become flexible again. Livor mortis is

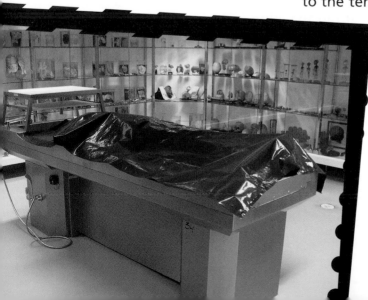

Dead bodies are put in sterile body bags before they are sent for post mortem.

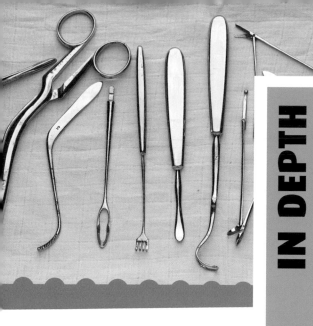

Pathologists use surgical instruments to carry out a post mortem.

Insect information

It may sound strange, but insects can provide information about the time of a person's death. Flies lay eggs on dead bodies. These hatch into maggots that mature into another generation of flies. More eggs are laid, and the process continues. Other insects, such as beetles, gather on a dead body later on. Studying the maggot generations, and identifying the different types of insect present, can help to determine when the person died. The scientists who carry out these investigations are called forensic entomologists.

the effect of gravity on the body. When the heart stops, the blood settles in the lower body parts and colours the skin like a bruise. These changes can help to pinpoint the time of death. Other signs are also considered, such as how much of the body has decomposed (rotted away).

Pathologists begin every post mortem with an external examination of the body. They make a note of everything they find. Marks on the body are photographed. They can provide clues about the victim's lifestyle or how he or she died. The body is also examined for trace evidence such as scrapings of skin under the fingernails.

Once the outside of the body has been fully examined, the internal examination begins. The pathologist makes a Y-shaped cut down the front of the body. The internal organs are removed and weighed. All the evidence is then sent to the laboratory for analysis.

Identifying the body

We all look different. Our face shapes are different, as is our skin colour. Individual features also distinguish us from each other. Some people have a unique mark such as a distinctive scar, tattoo or birthmark. Others may have a broken nose or unusually shaped ears. All of these things are carefully noted during a post mortem and used for identification.

8

Dental records

Sometimes it may not be possible to make a visual identification, particularly if the face of a body has decomposed or has been destroyed. In these cases, teeth can play a very important part in the identification of a body.

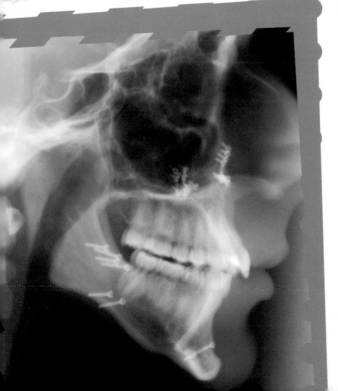

◀ *This X-ray shows metal pins inside the jaw. This type of information is especially useful when identifying a body.*

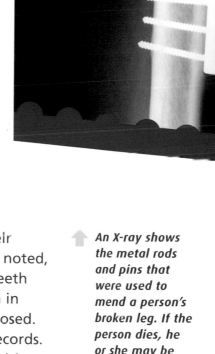

IN DEPTH

Sent to the lab

Samples of tissues and body fluids are sent to the laboratory after a post mortem. Forensic toxicologists analyse the chemicals in them. Chromatography is a method used to separate the chemicals. Mass spectrometry is a method used to identify each chemical. The results of these tests may be helpful to investigators. For example, they may show that the person was taking a medicine used to treat a particular illness. This type of information can help investigators to reveal the identify of an unknown person.

Dentists keep detailed records about their patients' teeth. Any that are missing are noted, as are fillings, crowns and other work. Teeth are durable and remain in the skull even in bodies that are badly burned or decomposed. Teeth can be compared against dental records. If a match is found, the police have a positive identification for the body. The person who does this is called a forensic odontologist.

An X-ray shows the metal rods and pins that were used to mend a person's broken leg. If the person dies, he or she may be identified by matching the old injury to X-ray records.

Old injuries often help to establish a person's identity. Investigators look for injuries such as a broken leg, which may have occurred years earlier. If the body is X-rayed and an injury matches one in medical records, this may establish the person's identity. Dental records or fingerprints will confirm the identification.

Facts from bones

Forensic anthropologists examine bones to obtain evidence about the person. Bones can tell them about the person's age, sex, ancestry, height, build and any injuries that occurred either before or around the time the person died. Bones may also provide additional information, such as whether the person was right- or left-handed and what activities they routinely did.

Finding the skull may be crucial to a forensic investigation.

Facial reconstruction

A skull is the scaffolding of a face. A forensic artist can use it to create an image of what the person looked like. He or she may draw a flat, two-dimensional (2-D) picture, or make a three-dimensional (3-D) model. This process is called facial reconstruction.

3-D model

Forensic artists first examine the skull for clues such as bumps and marks.

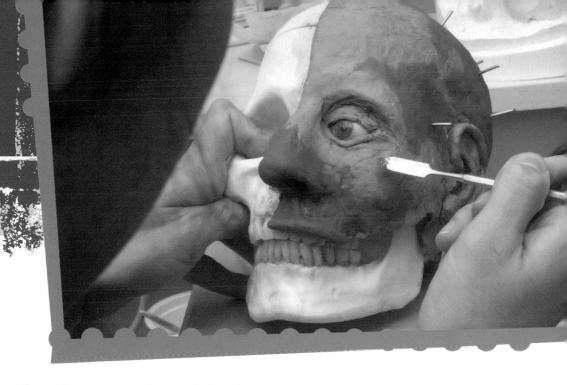

A forensic artist adds details to a facial reconstruction.

They also measure it carefully. The skull itself cannot be used as a base for the model, so the artist makes a copy of it. To do this, false eyes are put into the eye-sockets and the nose hole is blocked with clay. The skull is then covered with a rubbery substance. When this substance hardens, it is removed from the skull and used as a mould. Plaster is poured into the mould and left to set until it is hard.

Positional pegs are attached to points on the skull. These guide the artist and help him or her create the features accurately. Clay is applied to the cast, building up the face and then the nose and lips. The area around the eyes is refined, and the ears are moulded. Finally, details such as the hair and wrinkles are added.

TRUE CRIME...

Art catches criminal

In June 1996, a farmer found a body in a grave in his field in Hampshire. There were few clues about the dead person's identity, so police turned to a forensic artist, Richard Neave, who used the skull to reconstruct the face of the dead man. The victim was identified on the BBC *Crimewatch* programme. The name of the victim, Harjit Singh Luther, led the police to the murderer – Balijeet Singh Rai. To stay in Britain, Balijeet had married Harjit's wife. He killed Harjit fearing he would find out. Balijeet was sentenced to life imprisonment for the murder.

Creating faces with computers

Some modern forensic artists use computers to generate images from skulls. The skull is set on a rotating turntable. As it turns, it is scanned with a colour laser scanner. Measurements are then recorded from every angle. The computer software uses these to calculate the distances between many points on the skull. The computer generates a network that looks rather like a wire frame. This is rotated so that it can be viewed from different angles.

IN DEPTH

Close likeness

There are limitations to facial reconstructions. Although a drawing, model or computer image may look sufficiently like the person for the purposes of identification, it is unlikely to look exactly like him or her. This is because some details have to be guessed. Unless hair has been found with the body, for example, the forensic artist will not know what it was like. The shapes of the nose and ears can also only be guessed.

The next step

Muscle and skin are added to the skull. The forensic artist uses scans of living people that record 3-D information about bones and flesh. The artist selects someone whose skull is similar to the skull in question. The two images are merged to produce an image of the person's face. Details such as hair, skin and eye colour are added.

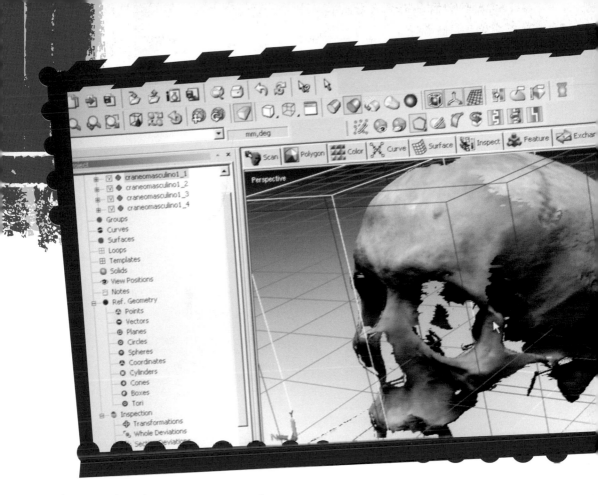

🔺 *Forensic artists use computer software to reconstruct the face of a person from his or her skull.*

To do this, a photograph of a living person of the same age, sex and ancestry as the skull is used. Computer software merges this picture with the previous image. The reconstructed face can be viewed on screen. The image can also be sent to other computers, or accessed via the Internet, so that everyone who needs to can see the picture.

Into the future

Future developments might include creating moving images of a reconstructed face. Also, a database containing facial details of missing persons may be created. Computerised images created from skulls could then be compared to the database records.

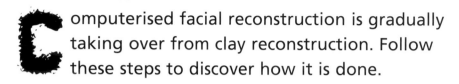

A face from a skull

Computerised facial reconstruction is gradually taking over from clay reconstruction. Follow these steps to discover how it is done.

1. The skull is placed on a turntable.

2. The turntable rotates. A laser scanner lights up a thin vertical stripe. Mirrors on either side of the turntable reflect images from the lit-up area to sensors.

3. The computer calculates the distances of each point on the skull. It uses this information to create a fully digitised model of the skull. The model looks like a network of wires and can be rotated on the computer monitor.

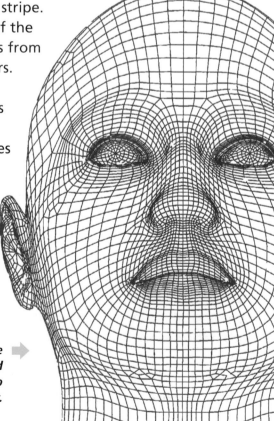

As the turntable rotates, a wire-frame matrix is generated. This digitised model of the skull is easy to manipulate on the computer.

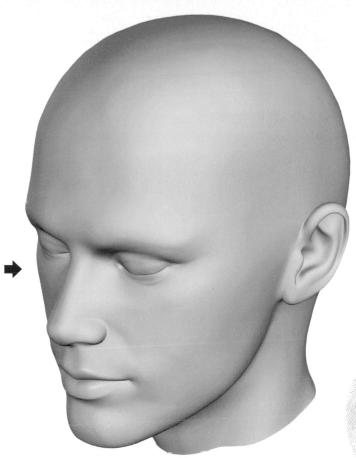

Once the frame of the skull has been created, forensic artists add details such as the ears and facial features.

4. A scan of the face of a living person is selected. The person needs to be of the same age, sex and ancestry as the person whose skull it is.

5. The scan of the living person is combined with the scan of the skull by superimposing one skull on top of the other. The two skulls are never exactly the same shape, so the computer software adjusts them both slightly until they match each other.

6. A photograph of the face of a person of similar age, sex and ancestry to the skull is selected. The computer combines this with the previous image. This adds detail such as skin colour, hair colour and texture.

7. The final reconstruction can be seen from different angles to get a complete view of the head.

Trace evidence

All the tiny things that might provide clues about a crime are called trace evidence. Trace evidence that comes from living things is called biological evidence. It includes hairs, skin, blood, body fluids, insects and plant material. Trace evidence that does not come from living things is called physical evidence. It includes broken glass, paint flakes and bullet holes.

Gathering evidence

Crime-scene investigators search for every scrap of trace evidence they can find. They wear special forensic body suits so that they do not contaminate the evidence. They work carefully so that nothing is damaged. Anything that might be useful is photographed. Investigators then collect evidence, using tweezers or a small artist's paintbrush to pick it up if it is small. They put it into a bag or container, label it and send it to the laboratory for analysis.

It is important that investigators do not overlook any piece of evidence. Even a tiny fibre could prove to be a valuable clue.

IN DEPTH

Hair analysis

A single hair can provide detailed information about a person. Chemicals from a person's food and drink can be found in his or her hair. Chemicals in drinking water supplies vary from place to place. Scientists analyse the minute amounts of some chemicals in hairs and then compare them with drinking water records. From this, they can tell where a person has been living.

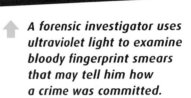

A forensic investigator uses ultraviolet light to examine bloody fingerprint smears that may tell him how a crime was committed.

This table shows some types of trace evidence and gives an example of where each might be found. It also shows the information that investigators may obtain from evidence.

Type of evidence	Where might it be found?	What might be learned from it?
footprint	hard floor	a person's shoe size; type of shoe worn
hair	cushion	colour and texture of a person's hair; where they lived; any drugs they had taken
paint	vehicle	paint type and colour of the object the vehicle had hit
tool mark	window frame	type of tool used to break into a building
fibres	carpet	type of fabric a person's clothes were made from
blood splashes	wall	identity of the person whose blood it is; direction of the blow that caused the wound

DNA evidence

DNA is the short name of the chemical deoxyribonucleic acid. Every living thing contains DNA. It has a complicated structure that works as a code. This code carries information from one generation to the next. It is your DNA that determines features such as the shape of your nose or the colour of your eyes, and whether your hair is curly or straight.

Unique DNA

Although most of the DNA is the same in every person, a small fraction is different. This means that each person's DNA is unique. Only your identical twin would have exactly the same DNA as you. This means that scientists can use DNA for identification.

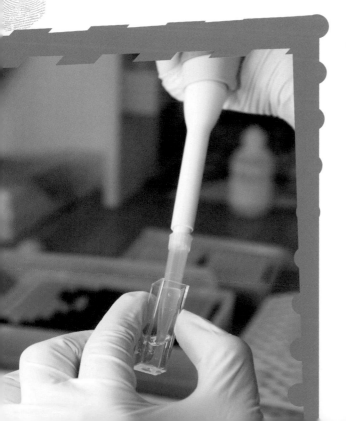

← *Evidence found at a crime scene is stored in a sterile container until it can be analysed.*

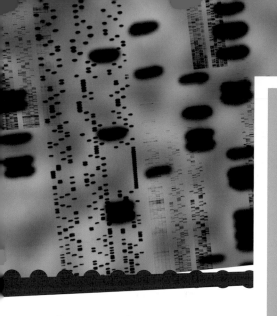

↑ *Processed DNA samples, called DNA fingerprints, look rather like barcodes.*

Using DNA

Evidence containing DNA is often found at a crime scene. Blood, bone, hair, fingernail clippings, skin, saliva and urine all contain DNA. Even tiny samples of biological material, such as saliva on a cigarette end, can contain enough DNA for analysis. DNA survives for a very long time. It can be extracted and analysed from old biological material, such as bones and teeth discovered many years after death. Once the sample has been collected from the crime scene, it is taken to the forensic laboratory. Then the process of analysis can begin.

Analysis of DNA samples can provide investigators with incredibly important information. It can help the police to identify people long after a crime has been committed. This may help to link a suspect to a crime scene, prove a suspect's innocence or identify a body.

IN DEPTH

Terrorist attacks

The terrorist attacks on the World Trade Center on 11 September, 2001 led to the largest use of DNA analysis for one event in history. Rescue workers gathered samples of bone and tissue from the site so that DNA could be taken and analysed in the hope of identifying victims. Scientists also analysed the DNA in medical samples and other items supplied by families who feared a relative may have died in the attack. By 2005, DNA analyses had helped to identify more than 1,592 out of the presumed 2,749 people who died. DNA analysis was also used to identify some of the 202 people who were killed following the bombing of a nightclub in Bali on 12 October, 2002. Recent advances allow DNA from smaller samples to be analysed. This means that further identifications should be possible in the future.

19

DNA markers

Scientists look for specific markers during the DNA analysis. If a DNA sample is matched with only one or two markers, the forensic investigators cannot be confident that their suspect committed the crime. A match of all the markers, however, is so rare that crime-scene investigators can be very confident that the suspect is guilty of the crime.

20

▲ *A forensic scientist compares the DNA fingerprint taken from DNA at a crime scene with records on a database.*

Processing DNA

The first step in DNA analysis is to separate the DNA from everything else in the sample using heat and a high-speed centrifuge. Then a chemical process makes copies of small sections of the DNA and separates them into individual groups. Special dyes and chemicals are added, which will show up when the DNA is analysed. When the chemical processes are complete, the DNA sample is seen as a pattern of dark and light stripes called a 'DNA fingerprint'. The patterns of different samples can be compared. If the patterns are identical, the samples must have come from the same person.

Comparing samples

In many cases, investigators compare the DNA from a sample found at a crime scene with DNA taken from a suspect. If the two match, it shows that the suspect was at the crime scene. In other cases, investigators may not have a suspect. DNA records of known criminals are kept on both national and international databases. The records can be compared with crime-scene samples. If a match is found, it may help investigators to identify the criminal. Although DNA evidence is widely regarded as being extremely reliable, mistakes can still be made.

DNA analysis must be carried out in a sterile environment so the evidence is not contaminated in any way.

DNA crime

The first criminal to be convicted using DNA evidence was Colin Pitchfork. In separate attacks during the 1980s, Pitchfork raped and murdered two girls – Lynda Mann and Dawn Ashworth – in Narborough, Leicestershire. At first, the police arrested a local youth, Richard Buckland, who confessed to the murder. Meanwhile, Alec Jeffreys, a scientist from the University of Leicester, had been developing DNA analysis techniques. Jeffreys used his technique to analyse body fluids found on the bodies of the two murder victims. The DNA profile showed that Buckland was not the murderer. However, it did match the DNA sample of local baker Colin Pitchfork. The police arrested Pitchfork, who was later given life imprisonment for the crimes.

21

Matching DNA samples

Sometimes DNA is the only thing that can link a criminal to the scene of a crime. Follow these steps to match a suspect's DNA with a crime-scene sample.

1. A crime-scene investigator carefully swabs the inside of a suspect's cheek to collect a DNA sample. It is put into a sterile container, and the container is labelled.

2. The DNA must be separated from everything else in the sample. This requires several laboratory processes, which are carried out until only the DNA itself remains. The processes used to extract DNA from a sample include heating the sample to 100°C (212°F) and spinning the sample in a high-speed centrifuge.

◀ *One of the easiest ways to collect a sample of DNA is to run a sterile swab around the inside of the suspect's mouth. The swab is then sealed in a tube and sent to a laboratory for analysis.*

A forensic scientist finds a match between DNA found at a crime scene and the suspect.

23

3. Small sections of the DNA are copied many times. Then the copies are separated into individual groups. Special dyes and chemical probes are added. These will show up when the DNA is analysed.

4. The DNA sections are examined. The exact method used to examine DNA depends on which dyes were added to the DNA sample.

5. A forensic scientist compares the suspect's DNA with the sample taken from the crime scene. The markers that the scientist looks at must be the same in both samples, and they must match exactly.

6. Success! The DNA match links the suspect directly to the crime scene. This is vital evidence that could be used to secure a conviction in court.

Looking at fingerprints

The skin on the fingertips has a distinct pattern of tiny ridges. Pressing a finger against a hard surface leaves a mark, called a fingerprint. Scientists think that fingerprints are unique. No two people – not even identical twins – have been found with the same print in more than 100 years that they have been used to identify people. This means that prints from a person can be used to match to prints taken from a crime scene.

Types of fingerprints

Not all fingerprints are alike because of the way in which they are made, or the surface upon which they are left. There are three main types.

1. Patent prints are made with fingers that have touched something wet or sticky, such as warm blood.

Your fingertips are covered in lots of tiny ridges that create a unique pattern when you touch something.

Print shapes

Fingerprints are made up from three basic shapes:

Loops cross the fingertip from side to side, curving around or up. Radial loops slope towards the thumb. Ulnar loops slope in the opposite direction to radial loops.

Whorls are circular or spiral patterns.

Arches slope up and down.

Each person's fingerprint has a unique arrangement of these shapes. One person might have a big whorl, while another might have several loops. Details like these can be used to match a print from a person to a print found at the crime scene.

If you touch something sticky and then touch a glass, you are certain to leave behind a patent print.

25

If a smooth surface, such as glass, is then touched, some of the sticky residue will be transferred to the surface of the glass. A fingerprint will be visible in the marks left on the glass. These types of print are easy to see and easy to photograph.

2. Latent prints are made from the natural oils in a person's skin. When someone touches something, traces of these natural oils are transferred from the fingers to the surface of the glass. These fingerprints are not usually visible to the naked eye. They show up when a special powder or chemical is applied to the surface. Once revealed, they can be photographed.

3. Impressed prints are left behind only when you touch something soft, such as a bar of soap, clay or wet paint. These fingerprints are usually visible and can be photographed easily.

Using fingerprints

Fingerprints have been used in criminal investigations for more than 100 years. A person's fingerprints are usually taken by making the person roll each finger over an ink pad and then pressing it onto paper. In the past, a suspect's fingerprints were taken and compared to prints found at a crime scene.

TRUE CRIME...

The McKie case

In 1997, a smudged print was found at a murder scene in a flat in Kilmarnock near Glasgow, Scotland. After analysis, the print was found to match the thumb of PC Shirley McKie, who was part of the team investigating the murder. PC McKie was on duty outside the flat, but the print was found inside the flat. That meant that PC McKie had gone into the flat unlawfully. McKie denied the print was hers, but no one believed her. Fingerprint evidence could not lie, could it? Eventually, McKie called in two American experts to examine the print. They showed that a mistake had been made, and the print did not belong to PC McKie. So fingerprint evidence may not be as failsafe as people think.

Speeding up the process

Comparing fingerprints manually was slow and time-consuming. Today, advances in technology have speeded up the process of fingerprint analysis. Fingerprints are often taken using ink and paper, but the prints are then scanned and stored as a digital image. Many prints are stored on a computer database, helping to speed up the process of identification.

This image of a fingerprint was created by a digital scanner.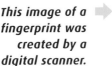

Digital scanner

Fingerprints can be recorded using a digital scanner. The suspect puts his or her finger on a glass screen. A digital image is taken in a similar way to a digital camera taking a picture. The details of the suspect are then stored on a database along with his or her prints. Other police forces can access the database information and the images of fingerprints of known criminals.

Sometimes, mistakes are made when analysing fingerprints. For example, a tiny but important difference between two sets of prints may be overlooked. This is a serious error that could lead to the wrong person being convicted of a crime.

EXAMINE THE EVIDENCE

Look at your own prints

Rub a soft pencil on a piece of paper. Press one of your fingertips onto the pencil mark. Now carefully stick a piece of clear adhesive tape on your fingertip. Pull it off slowly and stick it onto a piece of plain white paper. Your fingerprint will show up clearly. Ask a friend to do the same and compare the prints. Can you see any features that would distinguish each print? Wash your hands before you touch anything else!

Finding prints
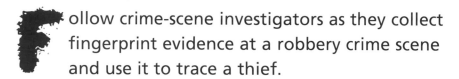

Follow crime-scene investigators as they collect fingerprint evidence at a robbery crime scene and use it to trace a thief.

1. A crime-scene investigator brushes black powder onto a door handle of an office that has been broken into. To begin with, she brushes in a circular motion. Then, when prints begin to become visible, she brushes in the same direction as the ridges of the prints.

2. A photographer takes pictures of each print. These provide a permanent record of the prints and may be produced as evidence in court.

3. An investigator also takes a copy of each print. He places clear adhesive tape over the print, then pulls off the tape and sticks it onto a piece of cardboard.

A record of a fingerprint can be made by placing clear adhesive tape over the print.

A crime-scene investigator brushes black powder onto a door frame to reveal the prints left on its surface.

The black lines of the print show up clearly on the card. Like the photographs, these copies provide a permanent record of the prints and may be used as evidence.

4. The photographic images are transferred onto a computer.

5. Investigators log on to a fingerprint identification system and database.

6. Computer software compares the images of the prints from the door handle with the database records. Investigators can view two sets of prints side by side on the screen to see if they are similar.

7. After comparing a large number of prints, a match is found. This links a man to the crime scene. It also means that the man has already committed a serious crime and the police can look up his criminal record. The police will find out the suspect's last known address so that they can trace him and question him about the robbery.

Speaking and writing

In some cases, evidence such as a recording of a voice or a written note can help investigators to identify someone.

Information from a voice

Studying a person's voice in relation to a crime is called forensic phonetics. For detailed phonetic analysis, an instrument known as a sound spectrograph is used. This produces graphs, called spectrograms, of the words that are spoken. Phonetic analysis can do two things:

1. It can provide information about a speaker. A person's voice provides information about his or her age and gender. A teenage girl will sound very different from an elderly man. Local accents can give a clue about where a person comes from. Clues about a person's ethnic and social background can also be picked up from his or her voice. Investigators can use this information to narrow down their range of suspects.

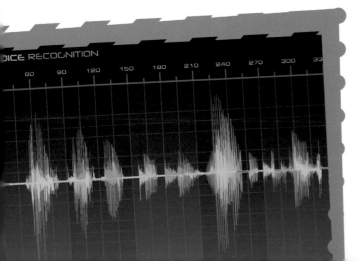

◀ *A spectrograph produces a graph like this one. The graph can provide vital clues about a suspect.*

A person's handwriting can reveal information about his or her personality and state of mind.

2. Not all tape-recordings are clear, and there may be a dispute about what was said. If a tape-recording of a police interview is not clear, the suspect may claim that he or she said one thing and the police another. A spectrograph can prove what was really said.

Looking at writing

A forensic document analyst may be able to tell if two documents were written by the same person. This cannot identify a person, but it may provide useful information.

A forensic document analyst will look at factors such as:

- the size of the letters
- whether the letters are upright or sloping
- whether the letter was written gently or with pressure
- the choice of words and phrases.

An Electrostatic Detection Apparatus (ESDA) test may be carried out. This reveals otherwise invisible evidence, such as added or altered words.

Finding the Ripper

In the 1970s and 1980s, a series of women were murdered in Yorkshire, England, by a man dubbed the 'Yorkshire Ripper'. Tapes were sent to the police by a man claiming to be the Ripper. An expert said the speaker on the tapes came from Wearside, in the northeast of England. Police switched their search to Wearside. The killings continued until a Yorkshireman called Peter Sutcliffe was arrested and then confessed to the murders. The tapes were a hoax. More than 25 years later, John Humble, from Wearside, admitted to sending the tapes. The voice analysis of the tape proved to be correct.

Investigative analysis

Investigative analysis provides police with information about a criminal's behaviour and personality. The information is put together using information about how a crime was committed. Creating a criminal profile is part of this process. A criminal profile gives a general description of the sort of person the police should be looking for.

Creating a profile

The profiling process has five main stages:

1. First, profilers collect as much information as possible about the crime. This includes evidence from the crime scene, photographs, post-mortem reports and witness testimonies.

2. Next, the information is organised into questions such as:
- What sort of crime was committed?
- Where was the crime committed?
- What was the main motive for the crime?
- How much risk did the criminal take?
- What did the criminal do before and after the crime?

3. Using the answers to these questions, profilers can begin to reconstruct the criminal's behaviour. They might also predict whether the criminal is likely to have known the victim and whether the crime was planned or carried out on an impulse.

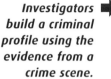

Investigators build a criminal profile using the evidence from a crime scene.

4. Profilers can now build up a description of the most likely sort of suspect. This would include the criminal's race, sex and age. It would also include whether or not they are married, what sort of place they live in and if they have a job. It may record their possible beliefs and values, and whether they are likely to have carried out similar crimes before.

5. The profiler passes his or her information to the detectives. They can use this to narrow down a list of suspects to individuals matching the profile.

If the profile is successful, a suspect may be identified, arrested, tried and found guilty.

EXAMINE THE EVIDENCE

33

Create your profile

Imagine that a profiler walked into your bedroom. What information could he or she find out about you? If you have a bookshelf, for example, perhaps the titles of the books would give a clue about your interests. Pictures on your walls might suggest what sort of music, dance, sport or animals you like. Your clothes and shoes might tell the profiler how tall you are. Stand in your room and pretend you have never seen it before. How much information can you collect about yourself? Can you build up a detailed profile?

Profiling history

The idea of criminal profiling is not a new one. Some investigators tried to develop a similar approach more than 200 years ago. However, their attempts were unsuccessful. It was not until the 1940s that police forces began to see that profiling could be a useful tool. After that, criminal profiling methods developed quickly.

▲ *Police and forensic scientists analyse evidence to identify a suspect.*

34

TRUE CRIME...

The Mad Bomber

In November 1940, an unexploded bomb was found in Manhattan in New York City. Over the next few years, similar bombs were found in other places in New York. The person responsible became known as 'The Mad Bomber of New York'. The police asked a forensic psychiatrist, named Dr James A. Brussel, to help them find the Mad Bomber. Dr Brussel used the bomber's letters and other evidence to build up a profile. The profile described the bomber as an unmarried man between 40 and 50 years old, who lived with a female relative. He was neat, educated, religious and probably European. It even suggested that he would be wearing a double-breasted suit with the buttons done up. Police eventually arrested George Metetsky, who confessed to the crimes. Metetsky was unmarried, 54, Polish and lived with his sisters. Even his suit matched the description in the profile!

Profiling units

Criminal profiling is also called offender, or psychological, profiling and criminal investigative analysis. Criminal profiling units have been set up across the world to compile profiles.

The first unit was set up in the United States in the 1950s. It is known as the Behavioral Science Unit, and it is part of the Federal Bureau of Investigation (FBI).

The unit was established by Howard Teten and Pat Mullany. It later became the Investigative Support Unit, which is part of the National Center for the Analysis of Violent Crime (NCAVC). Initially, it was set up because of concern about the number of murders being carried out. Among its staff are mental health consultants and experts in behavioural or forensic science. The unit has collected a great amount of data about the behaviour of different types of criminal. The Investigative Support Unit is divided into departments that focus on different crimes. Unit One concentrates on counterterrorism, Unit Two deals with crimes against adults and Unit Three looks at crimes against children.

In Europe, Interpol (the International Criminal Police Organisation) set up the Analytical Criminal Intelligence Unit (ACIU) in 1993. This allowed Interpol to use profiling to help its member countries combat crime. Many individual countries within Europe also have their own national units

35

The FBI's Behavioral Science Unit is part of the National Center for the Analysis of Violent Crime (NCAVC).

FEDERAL BUREAU OF INVESTIGATION

Evidence from witnesses

In some cases, one or more people see a crime being carried out. They may catch a glimpse of the criminal's face. Often, they do not see the whole face or are too far away to see a lot of detail. However, forensic artists can use information from a witness to put together a portrait of the person.

In the past, forensic artists sketched a face from a description provided by a witness. The sketch could be used to track down the criminal. Some forensic artists still work in this way.

⬇ *Modern computer programs can change individual features at the touch of a button.*

Police use computerised Identi-Kits to make television appeals.

EXAMINE THE EVIDENCE

Make your own Identi-Kit

You will need paper, a pencil and some scissors. Draw outlines of several faces. Then draw several different hairstyles that would fit the heads. Draw several sets of eyes and ears, and several noses and mouths. Cut out the features. Choose one set of eyes, one set of ears and one nose. Put the features on your outlined face. Then experiment by changing eyes, noses and ears. Even if you have just four types of each facial feature, you can make up 4,096 different faces!

37

Identi-Kit

During the 1950s, the Identi-Kit was developed. This was a system of building a portrait from several witness statements. The original Identi-Kit included clear sheets, called 'foils', that showed different types of hand-drawn facial features. A witness could select the correct features. By stacking the clear foils on top of each other, a complete portrait was created. In later versions, photographs replaced the drawings. A computerised version is now available. A portrait of a face that approximately matches the description is shown on a screen. Witnesses can alter features one at a time until they are happy that the portrait matches the face that they saw. The final portrait is stored on the computer and can be accessed by police departments worldwide on the Internet.

Criminal databases

computers have revolutionised many aspects of forensic science. Investigators now have access to criminal records at the touch of a keyboard or click of a mouse. This means that searching records can be done in minutes or hours rather than the days or weeks it took to search paper records. Information can be made available to other police departments immediately using the Internet, rather than waiting for a fax, telegram or letter to be sent.

38

Criminals can be identified in an instant with the use of computer databases.

DNA databases worldwide

Records are held in different ways in different countries. In Britain, the National DNA Database (NDNAD) stores DNA records from samples collected at crime scenes and from individuals who have been arrested. It also stores other information, such as fingerprints. The British database is bigger than that of any other country. The information stored on the database helps police to identify offenders quickly and make arrests. In the United States, the National Crime Information Center (NCIC) has a database holding information about criminal records, escaped prisoners, stolen property and missing persons. The database can be accessed by police and other law-enforcement officers at any hour of the day or night.

Interpol's records

Interpol is the world's largest international police organisation, with 186 member countries. The organisation's headquarters are in Lyon, France. Interpol maintains databases that contain detailed information such as fingerprints, criminal records and photographs of known international criminals and alleged criminals. It also maintains databases about stolen documents and other property, stolen vehicles, missing persons and images showing the sexual abuse of children. The information is provided by the police forces from member countries. Each police force can access the databases and find information from police forces in other countries. Putting together information from several countries can help to identify criminals.

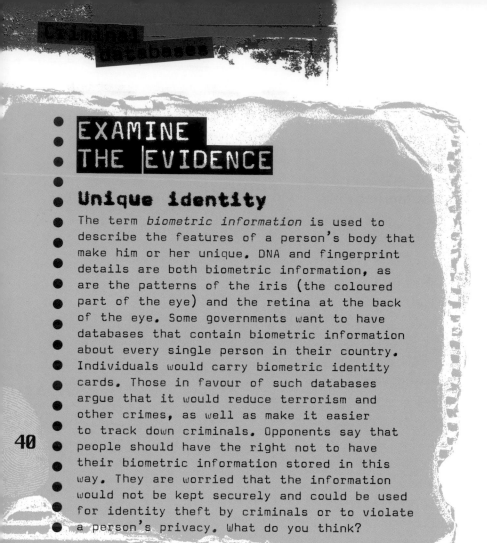

EXAMINE THE EVIDENCE

Unique identity

The term *biometric information* is used to describe the features of a person's body that make him or her unique. DNA and fingerprint details are both biometric information, as are the patterns of the iris (the coloured part of the eye) and the retina at the back of the eye. Some governments want to have databases that contain biometric information about every single person in their country. Individuals would carry biometric identity cards. Those in favour of such databases argue that it would reduce terrorism and other crimes, as well as make it easier to track down criminals. Opponents say that people should have the right not to have their biometric information stored in this way. They are worried that the information would not be kept securely and could be used for identity theft by criminals or to violate a person's privacy. What do you think?

40

Specific databases

Individual countries also maintain databases that hold information about one particular type of crime. In Britain, the Violent and Sex Offenders Register (ViSOR) holds details of people convicted of violent or sexual offences. The register helps to keep track of offenders who are released from prison. It is intended to reduce the chances of similar offences being committed. In the United States, each state maintains a database of sexual offenders, and these are co-ordinated by the FBI's National Center for the Analysis of Violent Crime.

Restricted access

There are security measures to protect the information held on criminal databases. Strict systems are in place to ensure that only authorised people can access the data. These systems include physical features such as alarms and locks, as well as computer controls such as the use of passwords and the storage of data in code.

Some people think that the public should have access to some types of database records. For example, parents may want to know whether there is a sex offender living near them and their children. In the United States, legislation called Megan's Law gives the public access to this information. In other countries, including Britain, this information is not released.

Database security breach

In 2003, an FBI agent pleaded guilty to unauthorised access of an FBI database. Originally from Lebanon, Nada Nadim Prouty had given false information about herself to get a job at the FBI's field office in Washington DC. She was not authorised to search the FBI database. While working there during 2002, however, Prouty searched the database for information about her relatives in Lebanon. A review of the security systems was undertaken to avoid a similar breach of security in the future.

41

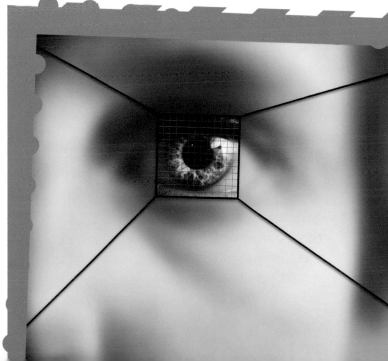

In some countries, iris recognition systems are used in airports.

Identifying groups

Not all crimes are committed by a single person. Small groups are responsible for some crimes. Other crimes are carried out by large groups of criminals and may involve more than one country.

Surveillance

Groups of people can plan and carry out a wide range of different offences such as drug smuggling, fraud and terrorism. Some organisations concentrate on a particular type of illegal activity, while others can be involved in many different crimes. Police must identify the members of the group to protect the public from their crimes.

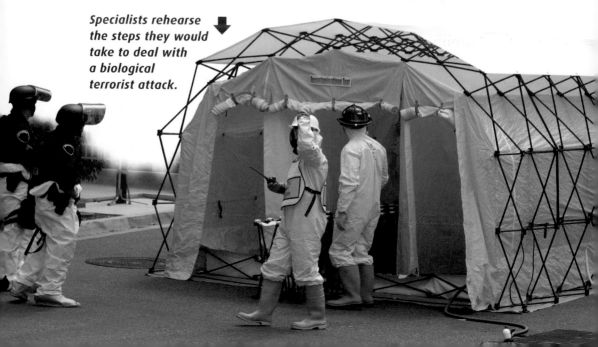

Specialists rehearse the steps they would take to deal with a biological terrorist attack.

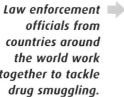

Law enforcement officials from countries around the world work together to tackle drug smuggling.

Identifying the members of a large criminal organisation may involve months or years of surveillance. Initially, only minor members of the group may be identified and their movements monitored. The information obtained may help investigators to identify more important group members. Police can then arrest the entire group, rather than just an individual.

Working together

Police forces from across a country sometimes work together to solve group crimes. Interpol, the FBI and police forces from many countries may join forces for international investigations. These will often involve other officials, for example customs and immigration.

TRUE CRIME...   43

Anthrax attack

Some dangerous biological materials are stored in many laboratories around the world. Some laboratories have samples of a microbe that causes a deadly disease called anthrax. Despite high security levels, the microbes may find their way into the hands of criminals. In the United States in 2001, letters containing anthrax spores were sent to two senators and several news organisations. Five people died and 17 others were infected with anthrax. Over the next seven years, the FBI narrowed down their search to one suspect, Dr Bruce Ivins. Ivins committed suicide in 2008 before he could be convicted of the crime.

Careers in forensics

What would it be like to be involved in the identification process? This depends on which area of the subject you choose. Each type of specialist has unique training and working methods.

Crime-scene investigators

Crime-scene investigators (CSIs) collect the clues that forensic experts analyse. Most CSIs start out as police officers before training to be a CSI. Increasingly, a university degree is needed to become a CSI. Chemistry and biology are two subjects that police look for in their CSIs. CSIs pass information to other specialists such as forensic pathologists and toxicologists. Each expert then uses his or her own particular expertise to help in the identification process.

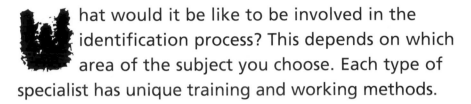

SALARY CHART

This chart shows how much some forensic scientists working in criminal investigations can expect to earn.

Forensic scientist	Approximate salary per year
Crime-scene investigator	£40,000
Forensic pathologist	£47,000
Forensic artist	£38,000

Forensic pathologists

Forensic pathologists are doctors who have special training to carry out post mortems. It takes many years of study and a lot of skill to become a forensic pathologist. This fascinating job plays an invaluable part in the field of forensics.

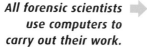
All forensic scientists use computers to carry out their work.

Forensic artist

To be a successful forensic artist, you need to be able to draw accurately and create sketches from spoken and written descriptions. Some formal art training is usually needed, and some specialised forensic art courses are available. A basic knowledge of anatomy is helpful for tasks such as facial reconstructions.

Other jobs

For most careers involved with forensic identification, you need some basic skills. These include:

- being able to work accurately
- being methodical and logical in the way you work
- being competent at mathematics and computing
- being able to write clearly and accurately
- a detailed understanding of one or more basic science subjects.

If this sounds like you, why not think about forensic science as a career? Many universities offer special degrees in forensic science. Other colleges offer shorter courses in a single area of forensic science.

Glossary

algor mortis – When a dead body cools to the surrounding temperature.

biometric – Describes the biological features of a person, such as DNA and fingerprints.

database – Collection of information, usually stored on a computer.

DNA – Genetic material that carries the code that determines the make-up of every living thing

DNA fingerprint – Individual record created from DNA that can be stored on databases and used to identify someone in a criminal case.

fibre – Fine strand of material.

forensic anthropologist – Scientist who studies the origin and development of human beings.

forensic artist – Person who creates portraits based on forensic evidence.

forensic entomologist – Scientist specialising in the study of insects that feed on dead bodies.

forensic ondontologist – Scientist specialising in the study of dental evidence in a crime.

forensic scientist – Person who uses science and technology to investigate and establish facts in a criminal case.

forensic toxicologist – Scientist who deals with poisons and their effect, and the problems involved.

laser – Device that creates an intense beam of light.

livor mortis – Blood settling in a dead body thanks to the force of gravity.

organs – Parts of the body, such as the heart, lungs and brain.

pathologist – Doctor who studies human remains to help work out the cause of death.

perpetrator – Person who commits a crime.

phonetics – Study of the way in which people speak.

post mortem – Examination of a dead body to find out the cause of death.

profiling – Building up a picture of criminals from the evidence found at crime scenes.

rigor mortis – Stiffness of the body for a period of hours after death.

saliva – Liquid produced by glands in the mouth to keep it moist.

sterile – Completely clean.

surveillance – Watching and recording a person's movements.

ultraviolet – Type of light invisible to our eyes, with wavelengths shorter than visible violet or blue light.

X-rays – Energetic rays that can pass through substances that rays of light cannot penetrate.

Further reading

Books

Cooper, Chris. *Forensic Science.* London: Dorling Kindersley, 2008.

Dowen, Elizabeth. *What's it Like to be a Forensic Scientist?* London: A & C Black Publishers, 2009.

Parker, Steve. *Fingerprint Wizards.* London: A & C Black Publishers, 2009.

Platt, Richard. *Forensics.* London: Kingfisher, 2008.

Rose, Malcolm and Hill, Dave. *Scene of the Crime: A Forensic Mystery Where You Crack the Case.* London: Kingfisher, 2008.

Websites

Find out how crime scene investigations work at the How Stuff Works website:

http://science.howstuffworks.com/csi.htm

There is lots of information about forensic science and crime-scene investigations, plus a mystery to solve at:

www.abc.net.au/science/slab/forensic/default.htm

There is a database of forensic science facts, a timeline showing important forensic events and a game to play at:

www.virtualmuseum.ca/Exhibitions/Myst/en/rcmp/index.html

Index